A Tractor's Day

by Lily Schell
Illustrated by Mike Byrne

 BELLWETHER MEDIA
MINNEAPOLIS, MN

Blastoff! Missions takes you on a learning adventure! Colorful illustrations and exciting narratives highlight cool facts about our world and beyond. Read the mission goals and follow the narrative to gain knowledge, build reading skills, and have fun!

Traditional Nonfiction

Narrative Nonfiction

Blastoff! Universe

MISSION GOALS

> FIND YOUR SIGHT WORDS IN THE BOOK.

> LEARN ABOUT WHAT A TRACTOR DOES ON A FARM.

> IDENTIFY THREE DIFFERENT PARTS OF A TRACTOR.

This edition first published in 2023 by Bellwether Media, Inc.

No part of this publication may be reproduced in whole or in part without written permission of the publisher. For information regarding permission, write to Bellwether Media, Inc., Attention: Permissions Department, 6012 Blue Circle Drive, Minnetonka, MN 55343.

Library of Congress Cataloging-in-Publication Data

Names: Schell, Lily, author.
Title: A tractor's day / by Lily Schell.
Description: Minneapolis, MN : Bellwether Media, Inc., 2023. | Series: Blastoff! Missions. Machines at work | Includes bibliographical references and index. | Audience: Ages 5-8 | Audience: Grades 2-3 |
Summary: "Vibrant illustrations accompany information about the different jobs a tractor has. The narrative nonfiction text is intended for students in kindergarten through third grade"-- Provided by publisher.
Identifiers: LCCN 2022013755 (print) | LCCN 2022013756 (ebook) | ISBN 9781644876640 (library binding) | ISBN 9781648348488 (paperback) | ISBN 9781648347108 (ebook)
Subjects: LCSH: Farm tractors--Juvenile literature.
Classification: LCC S711 .S28 2023 (print) | LCC S711 (ebook) | DDC 631.3/72--dc23/eng/20220411
LC record available at https://lccn.loc.gov/2022013755
LC ebook record available at https://lccn.loc.gov/2022013756

Text copyright © 2023 by Bellwether Media, Inc. BLASTOFF! MISSIONS and associated logos are trademarks and/or registered trademarks of Bellwether Media, Inc.

Editor: Derek Zobel   Designer: Andrea Schneider

Printed in the United States of America, North Mankato, MN.

This is **Blastoff Jimmy**! He is here to help you on your mission and share fun facts along the way!

Table of Contents

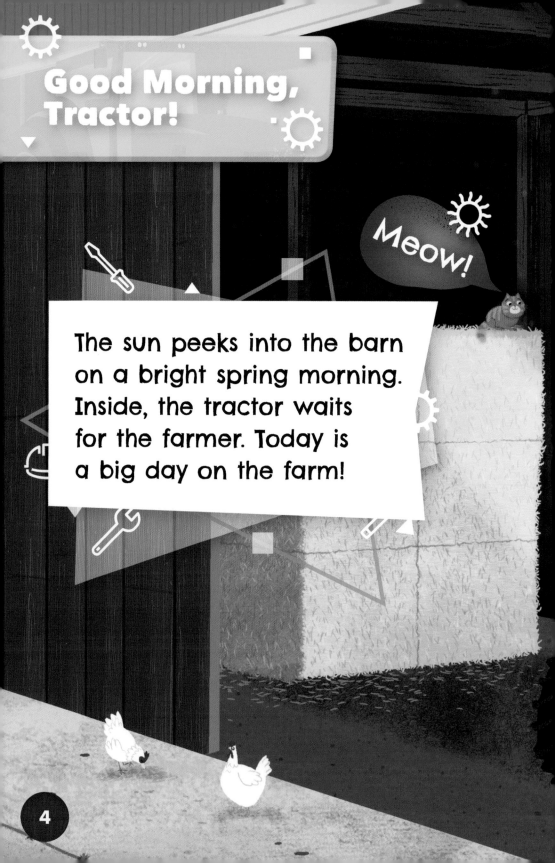

Good Morning, Tractor!

Meow!

The sun peeks into the barn on a bright spring morning. Inside, the tractor waits for the farmer. Today is a big day on the farm!

barn

Last fall, the tractor helped prepare the ground for spring planting. It pulled a heavy **plow** through the long, wide fields.

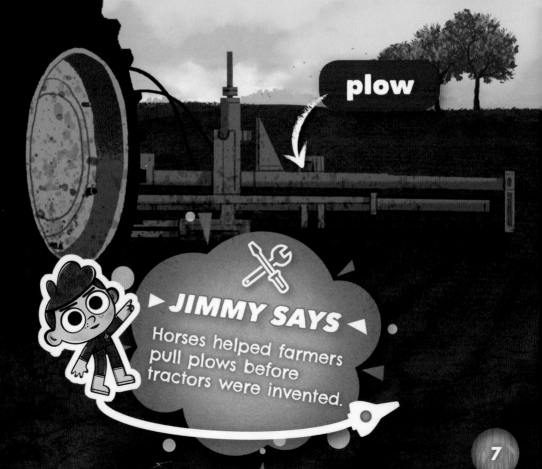

plow

Planting Corn

cab

Today, the tractor will help plant corn. The farmer enters the barn and climbs into the tractor's **cab**. Ready to go!

9

The **engine** rumbles as
the farmer starts the tractor.

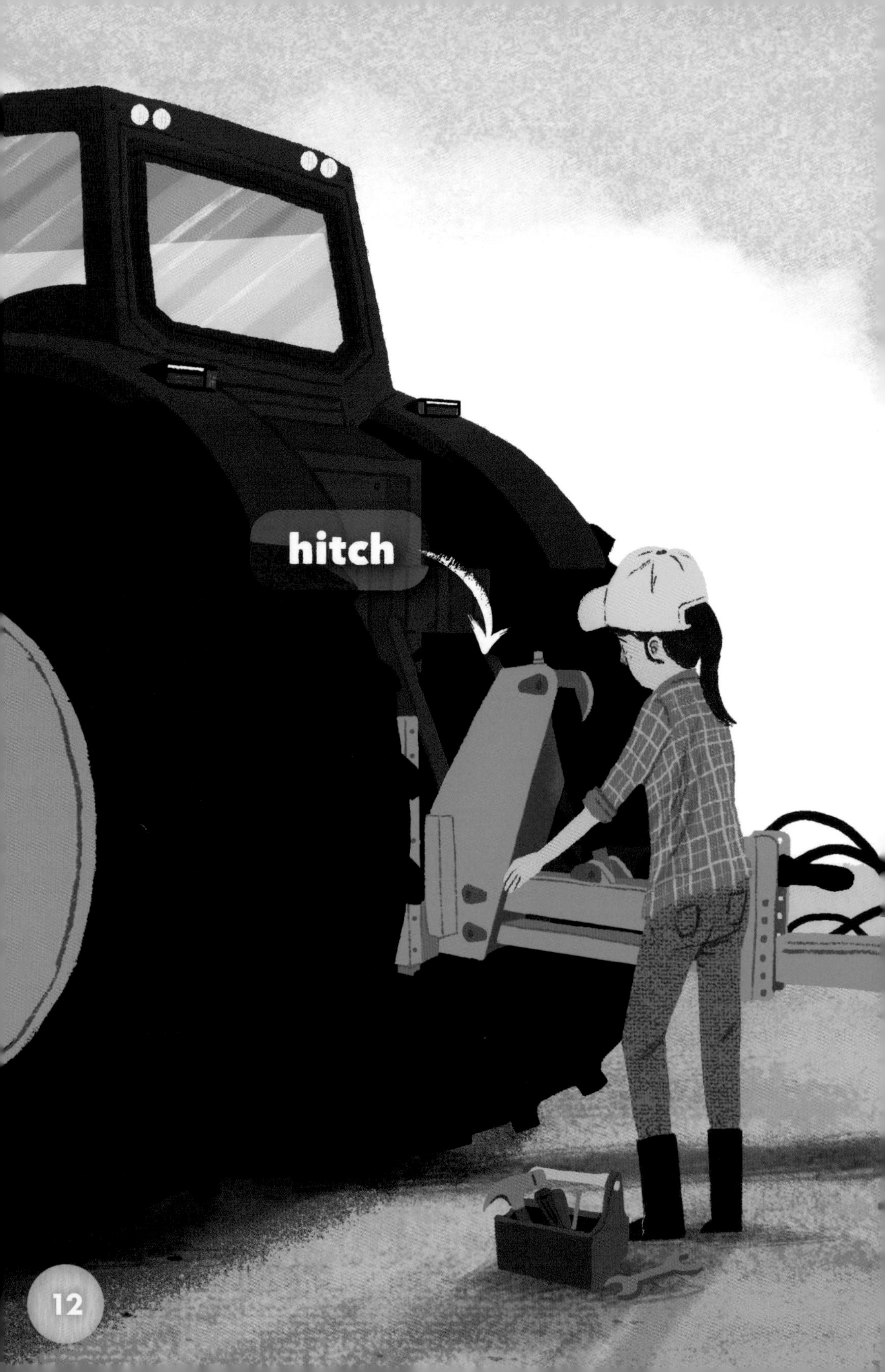
hitch

The farmer stops once they are outside. She backs up to a big tool and hooks it to the tractor's **hitch**. This is the **planter**.

planter

The tractor drives in neat lines through the field. It pulls the planter behind it.

seed

The planter drops seeds into the earth. Corn will grow from them.

The ground is muddy.
But the tractor does not slip.
Treads on its big tires
dig into the soft land.

▶ **JIMMY SAYS** ◀

Some tractor tires
are more than 7 feet
(2 meters) tall!

treads

Finally, the job is done. The farmer steers the tractor back to the barn. She sprays the mud off of its big tires. Then, she drives it inside.

In a few months, the tractor will help **harvest** the corn. It has a lot of jobs to do on the farm!

Tractor Jobs

prepare the ground

plant seeds

harvest crops

Glossary

cab–the place where the driver sits

engine–the part of a tractor that makes it go

harvest–to gather a crop when it is done growing

hitch–a part on a tractor that connects it to other tools

planter–a tool that connects to a tractor to help plant seeds

plow–a tool that digs into soil to get it ready for planting

treads–bumps on tires that help them grip the ground

To Learn More

AT THE LIBRARY

Carr, Aaron. *Tractors*. New York, N.Y.: AV2, 2022.

Oachs, Emily Rose. *Tractors*. Minneapolis, Minn.: Bellwether Media, 2017.

Rossiter, Brienna. *Big Machines on the Farm*. Lake Elmo, Minn.: Focus Readers, 2021.

ON THE WEB

FACTSURFER

Factsurfer.com gives you a safe, fun way to find more information.

1. Go to www.factsurfer.com.

2. Enter "tractors" into the search box and click 🔍.

3. Select your book cover to see a list of related content.

BEYOND THE MISSION

> IF YOU HAD A TRACTOR, WHAT WOULD YOU PLANT? WHY?

> MAKE UP A NEW TOOL TO ATTACH TO THE TRACTOR'S HITCH. WHAT DOES IT DO? HOW DOES IT WORK?

> WHAT IS ONE NEW FACT YOU LEARNED FROM THE BOOK?

Index